A little Guide to

L I F E

by Purple Ronnie

First published 2002 by Boxtree
an imprint of Pan Macmillan Ltd
Pan Macmillan, 20 New Wharf Road, London N1 9RR
Basingstoke and Oxford
Associated companies throughout the world
www.panmacmillan.com

ISBN 0 7522 2041 1

9 8 7 6 5 4 3 2 1

A CIP catalogue record for this book is available from
the British Library.

Text by Giles Andreae
Illustrations by Janet Cronin
Printed and bound in Hong Kong

groove

Stress

If you get stressed out - dance until your pants explode

Tip for Boys

When girls get together
-it is best for boys
not to listen

Make Friends

Even being rich and sexy is useless if you haven't got any friends

Drinking

Beware:- Everyone looks sexy when you've got your beer goggles on

Perfect Men

All girls know there is no such thing as a Perfect Man

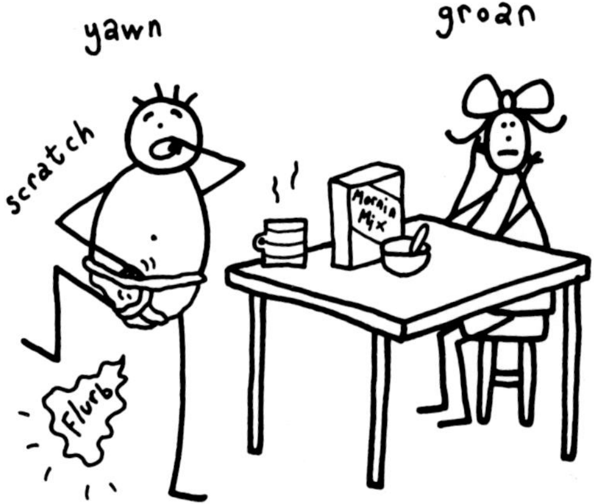

yawn
groan
scratch
Mornin Mix
Flurb

Sneaky Tip

Some people can always find ways to escape the washing up

Tip for Men

It's not what you've got that counts - it's what you can do with it

knowing you're In Love

You know you're
In Love when your
whole body wants to
explode with
happiness

Friendship

Some friends stay
with you wherever
you go

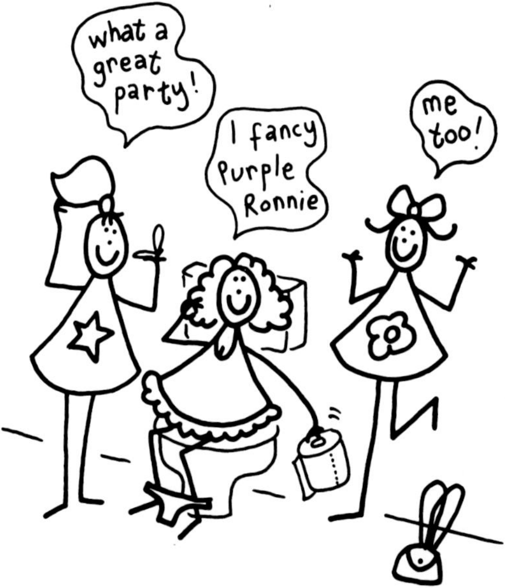
what a great party!
I fancy Purple Ronnie
me too!

Warning about Girls

Never get in between a girl and her chocolate

Important Tip

Tidy people do not always make the best lovers

Pants

You can always tell
what people are like
from the pants they
wear

☆

<u>Sneaky Tip for Men</u>

Girls like it when you show how much you love them in front of their friends

<u>Being Gorgeous</u>

Some people are so gorgeous that it doesn't matter what they say

Chatting Up Girls

Beware :- Not all girls like the same chat up lines

<u>Hugging</u>

Everybody needs a hug from time to time

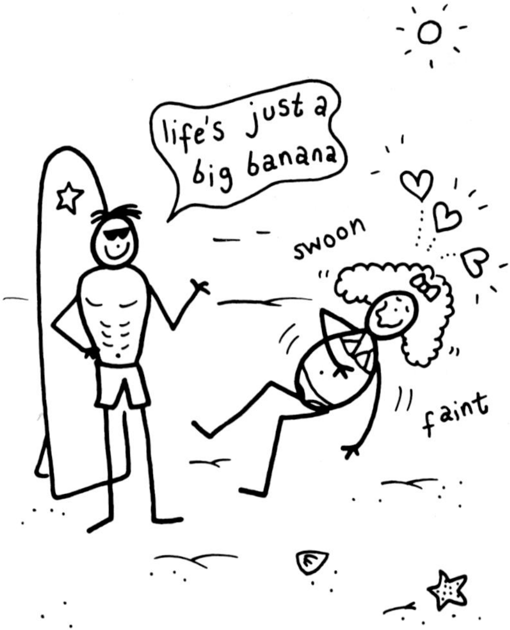
life's just a big banana
swoon
faint

Warning about Bosoms

A nice pair of bosoms can turn grown-up men into dribbling babies

Solving Problems

Men have a brilliant way of solving all their problems

Special Tip about Girls' Bottoms

When a girl asks you about her bottom you must <u>always</u> say it looks fantastic

Going to the Lav

Remember – Nothing

is more satisfying
than a really good
session on the lav

Getting Pissed

Warning:- Never get **too** pissed if you want to Do It

Girls and their Clothes

However many clothes a girl has got - she can never find the right thing to wear